Worship Booklet for Pilgrims

Third Edition

UPPER
ROOM BOOKS®
NASHVILLE

The Walk to Emmaus Worship Booklet for Pilgrims, Third Edition
Copyright © 2008 by Upper Room Books
All rights reserved.

Upper Room Books® website books.upperroom.org

Scripture quotations are from the New Revised Standard Version Bible, © copyright 1989 Division of Christian Education of the National Council of the Churches of Christ in the United States of America. Used by permission. All rights reserved.

Apostles' Creed, Ecumenical Version. Used by permission of the English Language Liturgical Consultation. Revision of ICET Translation.

"The Sacrament of the Lord's Supper" (pp. 26–34) is an adaptation of *A Service of Word and Table* © 1972, 1980, 1985, 1989 The United Methodist Publishing House. Reprinted by permission.

"Whom Do You Trust?" (p. 41) was originally printed in *The Upper Room* magazine for use on June 21, 2001. "Now I Know" (p. 42) was originally printed in *The Upper Room* magazine for use on January 23, 2007. "Hold the Ladder" (p. 43) was originally printed in *The Upper Room* magazine for use on April 30, 2008. All these meditations are used by permission.

Cover design: Bruce Gore
Interior design: PerfecType, Nashville, TN

Printed in the United States of America

ISBN 978-0-8358-1512-3
E1512

The International Walk
to Emmaus Worship Booklet

Your name: _____

Community name: _____

Emmaus Walk #: _____ Date: _____

Event held at: _____

Lay Director: _____

Spiritual Director: _____

Table name: _____

Table leader: _____

Table members: _____

_____

_____

_____

_____

_____

_____

Contents

Invitation to a Spiritual Journey

The following prayer and scriptures will aid you during your Emmaus weekend as well as in all the days to follow. Nothing is more important than your time with God your creator; Jesus, your brother; and the Holy Spirit, your source of strength and direction.

We hope that you will use this booklet to become more intentional in your spiritual life—in your private and family devotions; in group reunions, at Emmaus gatherings, and on times of spiritual retreat. We pray that this booklet will help support your life of prayer, spiritual growth, study, and Christian action.

Prayer and Spiritual Growth

Prayer of Saint Francis of Assisi

Lord, make me an instrument of thy peace;
where there is hatred, let me sow love;
where there is injury, pardon;
where there is doubt, faith,
where there is despair, hope;
where there is darkness, light;
and where there is sadness, joy.

O Divine Master, grant that I may not so much seek
to be consoled as to console;
to be understood, as to understand;
to be loved, as to love;

for it is in giving that we receive;
it is in pardoning that we are pardoned,
and it is in dying that we are born to eternal life.

Psalm 100

Make a joyful noise to the LORD,
   all the earth.
Worship the LORD with gladness;
   come into his presence with singing.

Know that the LORD is God.
   It is he that made us, and we are his;
   we are his people, and the sheep of his pasture.

Enter his gates with thanksgiving,
   and his courts with praise.
   Give thanks to him, bless his name.

For the LORD is good;
   his steadfast love endures forever,
   and his faithfulness to all generations.

Scripture Passages on Prayer

Jesus Teaches Us to Pray

Matthew 5:43-45

Matthew 6:5-6, 9-13

Matthew 18:19-20

Matthew 21:22

Mark 11:22-26

Luke 18:1-8

John 15:7-8

John 16:23-24

When Jesus Prayed

Matthew 9:36-38

Mark 1:35

Luke 3:21-22

Luke 5:15-16

John 6:11, 23

The Prayers of Jesus

Matthew 11:25-26

Luke 22:14-20

John 11:41b-42

John 17:1-26

The First Days of the Church

Acts 1:23-26

Acts 2:41-47

Acts 9:1-18

Acts 13:1-3

Acts 20:28-36

Acts 22:17-21

Prayer Strengthens the Church

Romans 8:14-15

Ephesians 3:14-21

Ephesians 6:18-20

Philippians 1:18b-19

1 Timothy 2:1-4

Hebrews 13:15

James 1:5-8

1 John 5:13-15

Prayer as a Blessing

Romans 16:25, 27

Hebrews 13:20-21

The Greatest Commandment

Read Matthew 22:34-40.

Loving God, you love us—all of us—
    and ask, in return,
    that we love you with all our hearts and souls and
    minds.

Loving God, you love us—all of us—
    and ask, in return,
    that we love our neighbors as we love ourselves.

Loving God, you love us—all of us—
    and ask, in return,
    that we forgive and not hold grudges.

Loving God, you love us—all of us—
    and ask, in return,
    that we take up our cross and follow you.

And by your grace we will love and obey.

Let it be so, now and forever.
Amen.

Reflection/Action

Do I make time each day to witness for Christ?
Do I go to the places where Jesus went?
Do I love those whom Jesus loved?
Is Christ made visible in my life and actions?

Time for God

Read Ecclesiastes 3:1-15.

Loving God, I am reminded that there is a time
    for everything in life.
Help me to look at each day as a new opportunity to
    be your servant.
Allow me to see you in the lives of those who surround
    me.
Open my eyes to look at them as you do, with love
    and compassion, so I can give myself in love to them.

Blessed Jesus, as my journey continues,
I want you to be my companion.
Teach me to overcome my sinful thoughts,
    my pride, and my selfishness.
Open my heart to your forgiveness and strength.
Lift me when I fall. Carry me when I am weak.

Holy Spirit, take away any negative attitude.
Guide me into the way that leads to life.
Make me sensitive to your promptings—
    eager for the presence and power of sanctifying grace.
Allow me to be your ambassador wherever I go today.

In Jesus' name I pray. Amen.

Reflection/Action

How can I know God's will and God's timing for this day?
How does my discipleship connect to the body of Christ,
    the church?

From Death to Life

Read Colossians 3:1-14.

Gracious God, give me the power
   to set my heart on things above.
Help me to put to death the old nature,
   sexual immorality, impurity, lust, and greed.

By your Holy Spirit, enable me to put aside
   unholy words, deeds, and thoughts.

I want to die to self, that I might live in Christ.
Give me the new self you have promised,
   which is being renewed in the knowledge
     and image of God:
   in compassion, kindness, humility, gentleness,
     and patience.

Help me to forgive, that I might be forgiven.

Help me to love as I have been loved. Amen.

Reflection/Action

How can I, with the help of my accountability group, put to
   death the attitudes and actions that lead to death?
How do I intentionally put into action the things that
   lead to life?

Happiness and Fruitfulness

Psalm 1

Happy are those
   who do not follow the advice of the wicked,
or take the path that sinners tread,
   or sit in the seat of scoffers;
but their delight is in the law of the LORD,
   and on his law they meditate day and night.
They are like trees planted by streams of water,
   which yield their fruit in its season,
and their leaves do not wither.
In all that they do, they prosper.

The wicked are not so,
   but are like chaff that the wind drives away.
Therefore the wicked will not stand in the judgment,
   nor sinners in the congregation of the righteous;
for the LORD watches over the way of the righteous,
   but the way of the wicked will perish.

Reflection/Action

My future happiness and desire for God will grow as I
   learn to meditate on God's Word. Why would I
   continue in the company of the ungodly?
Will I follow the way to fruitfulness, perseverance, and
   spiritual power?

Remembering the Way of Salvation in Prayer

1. *Believe the biblical teaching* that you were created by God and made in the likeness of God; therefore, God has a unique plan and purpose for your life (Gen. 1:26-27, 31; Jer. 29:11-12).

2. *Acknowledge your need for God.*
   You cannot reach God by your own efforts or your own good living (Rom. 3:23).

3. *Recognize God's love for you.*
   God is seeking you. God demonstrated unconditional love on the cross (John 3:16).

4. *Count the cost!*
   Repentance means unconditional surrender of your life to the will of God in Jesus Christ (Rom. 6:12-14).

5. *Accept Jesus Christ and his forgiveness.*
   We are saved by grace through faith in Jesus Christ alone. When we believe in him and open the door of our hearts to him, he will give us the light we need to live a new life (John 12:44-50; Rom. 10:9-13; Rev. 3:20).

6. *Commit yourself totally.*
   Acknowledge Christ's leadership in your life. Place all you are and hope to be in his hands (John 14:15).

7. *Share Christ with others in word and deed.*
   We are called to make disciples in word and deed. What we do to other people is, in reality, what we do to Jesus (Matt. 28:18-20; 25:31-46).

Redeemer

R eady to catch me when I fall,
E ver attentive to my call.
D ying for me upon the cross,
E rasing away all my dross.
E ncouraging each step I take,
M ediating then for my sake.
E ver answering all my prayers,
R edeemer loves me and he cares.

R.A. Gilmore, 1/31/04, used with permission.

Psalm Prayer (Psalm 30)

Almighty God,
    free us from anxiety over what we cannot control.
Restore our deep trust in you so that we can always
    rejoice and be thankful. Amen

Psalm 30, adapted by Kyunglim Shin Lee, in *Upper Room Worshipbook* (Nashville: Upper Room Books, 2006), no. 253. Adaptation © 2006 Upper Room Books.

Psalm Prayer (Psalm 34)

O God, you are worthy of our praise.
With humble hearts we bow in awe
    of your great mercy toward us.
You are near to the brokenhearted.
You save us from all our troubles.
Holy is your name. Amen.

Psalm 34, adapted by Ginger Howl, in *Upper Room Worshipbook* (Nashville: Upper Room Books, 2006), no. 265. Adaptation © 2006 Upper Room Books.

Examination of Conscience

Leader: Please listen as if God were speaking directly to you. *(Pause.)*

My child, think about your attitudes and disposition. Have your thoughts, your desires, your words, and your actions been worthy of one of my apostles?

How have you handled your problems today? Have you fallen in the face of them? What was the reason? Think it over.

Think about the means of grace available to you, the ways that you may grow in my grace: morning and evening prayer, worship, Holy Communion, spiritual friends. Are you availing yourself of these means of grace? Could you be more attentive and receive more benefit?

How long has it been since you have visited your spiritual director? When will you go?

And what about your serving? Could you have been more generous, more courageous, more self-sacrificing, more cheerful?

What are the obstacles to grace in your life? Are you trying to remove those obstacles by yourself? Or are you depending upon my Spirit?

What about your time? Do you make the time to be a disciple? Listen to me. Isn't it true that you find time for the things that really interest you? I, who am your God, would almost be satisfied if you would treat me as well as you treat any of your friends.

As my disciple, what have you done today that I may be better known, that I may be better loved?

Are you with me or against me? At work in your profession or at recreation, have you been my disciple? Would you have been proud to have me accompany you through the day?

Remember that what wounds my heart most are the infidelities of the "faithful." *I count on you! On you!*

And you, on whom or what do you count? What is the source of your spiritual life?

My child, don't stop halfway. I search for your whole heart, your passion, your fire, your energy, and your surrender. A Christian has a right to be enthusiastic. If you want to be, you can be. Tell me honestly, are you willing to give your all? Are you willing to live in my grace? Everything depends on your really wanting to be my disciple.

Leader: Now speak to the Lord.

All:

I have sinned and fallen short of your grace. Today I put my trust in you, O Lord, and your mercy. Accept me in the company of your apostles, freely forgiving my offenses through Christ. Fill me with the Holy Spirit and the fire of your love. Amen.

The Apostles' Creed (Ecumenical Version)

I believe in God, the Father Almighty,
    creator of heaven and earth.

I believe in Jesus Christ, his only Son, our Lord,
    who was conceived by the Holy Spirit,
    born of the Virgin Mary,
    suffered under Pontius Pilate,
    was crucified, died, and was buried;
    he descended to the dead.
    On the third day he rose again;
    he ascended into heaven,
    is seated at the right hand of the Father,
    and will come again to judge the living and the dead.

I believe in the Holy Spirit,
    the holy catholic* church,
    the communion of saints,
    the forgiveness of sins,
    the resurrection of the body,
    and the life everlasting. Amen.

universal

Psalm 23

The LORD is my shepherd,
   I shall not want.
He makes me lie down in green pastures;
   he leads me beside still waters;
he restores my soul.
   He leads me in right paths for his name's sake.

Even though I walk through the darkest valley,
   I fear no evil;
for you are with me;
   your rod and your staff—they comfort me.

You prepare a table before me
   in the presence of my enemies;
you anoint my head with oil;
   my cup overflows.
Surely goodness and mercy shall follow me
   all the days of my life,
and I shall dwell in the house of the LORD
   my whole life long.

An Exercise in Spiritual Reading
(Lectio Divina)

Leader: Select a few verses of scripture and arrange for three readers. Form groups of four to eight people. Invite participants to get comfortable and center themselves. Then ask them to listen for a word or phrase that stands out for them.

1st *time:* One person reads the passage aloud twice, slowly and meditatively. Participants repeat the passage softly to themselves during one minute of silence. At the leader's signal, they take turns sharing their word or phrase. (Individuals may pass.)

2nd *time:* This time, pay attention to impressions from the Holy Spirit. What in this text moves or touches you? A second person reads the text aloud. After two minutes of silence, participants speak a sentence or two, perhaps beginning with "I hear . . . ,""I see . . . ," or "I sense . . ." (Individuals may pass.)

3rd *time:* This time, listen for the beckoning of God. A third person reads the text aloud. Everyone ponders the question "How is the Spirit calling you to respond in the next few days?" during three minutes of silence. At the leader's signal, group members talk about their sense of invitation. (Individuals may pass.)

Closing: Join hands and offer a brief prayer for the person on your right, that he or she would respond to the invitation received from God. The prayer may be spoken or silent. If silent, when you have finished your prayer, gently squeeze the hand of the person on your right to indicate that it is his/her turn to pray for the person on his/her right.

Study

Study can take many forms: reading, listening to Christian teachers, participating in Bible study or a small group, preparing to lead a class or small group. Christian study should begin and end with prayer. All Christians are called to study to show themselves to God "as one approved . . . rightly explaining the word of truth" (2 Tim. 2:15).

The call to Christian study is a call to be a lifelong learner. Growth in grace is a lifelong process, and study is an essential aspect of the Christian journey toward maturity. Your joy and faithfulness as a disciple depend on study.

Appropriate study resources can strengthen your personal spiritual life, the spiritual life of your family, the life of your local fellowship, and your mission as a disciple of Jesus Christ. The pages in this section provide a starting point. Many other ideas and resources are available. The most important sources of guidance are Christ's example and the Holy Spirit's leading. Jesus promised that those who ask will receive, those who seek will find, and to those who knock, the door will be opened. (See Matt. 7:7; Luke 11:10.)

Your Spiritual Life

Daily Devotion—What resources do you use for daily scripture reading and prayer? For help, consult your pastor, the Spiritual Director from your Emmaus Walk, or *The Upper Room* daily devotional guide. *The Upper Room* is available online at www.upperroom.org or toll free by calling 1-800-972-0433.

Prayer Life—What books on prayer have you read? How comfortable is your communication with God? How much time do you invest in prayer each day? When you pray, how much time do you spend speaking, and how much time listening? If God were leading you to learn new ways to pray, where would you go for help?

Worship—What resources help you grow in your personal worship? Jesus said the first and greatest commandment is, "You shall love the Lord your God with all your heart, and with all your soul, and with all your mind" (Matt. 22:37). At this stage in your life, how has your understanding of worship changed?

How can you connect your personal worship of God to the worship of God practiced in your family? How do your personal and family worship practices enhance the worship experiences in your local church?

Group Reunion or some other small group for spiritual growth and mutual accountability—You cannot experience the fullness God intends for you without a small group of spiritual friends who are also intentional in their discipleship. The Bible clearly states that we cannot make it alone. We need the support, nurture, correction, and guidance of other Christians.

Spiritual Retreat—Jesus developed a rhythm of time alone with God, time with a small group, and time in ministry to others. If times of spiritual retreat to be alone with God were important for Jesus, they are equally important for those of us who want to follow him.

Your Family Life

Reflect on your growing-up years. What spiritual practices were important to your family? What good memories and models can you keep or revive today? What bad memories or practices will you need to study to overcome?

What resources help you with meaningful and appropriate family worship, scripture study, and prayer? Do these resources meet your needs, or do you need to find new ones? In addition to books, magazines, Web sites, and friends, identify spiritual leaders or guides who can help you.

The Bible clearly teaches that the role and responsibility of the more mature (parents or grandparents) is to help the less mature (children or grandchildren) come to love God with all their heart and with all their soul and with all their might (Deut. 6:5). This is our mission as Christian adults. How are you doing in this mission? Do you need help? If not, give thanks to God and persevere. If you do need help, ask God for grace and guidance. Make this a priority and get the help and resources you need.

Your Ministry in the Local Church

The Walk to Emmaus has provided you with a thorough review of the importance of the sacraments of baptism and the Lord's Supper. Through baptism, each Christian is marked as a child of God and given both grace and spiritual gifts for service (see 1 Cor. 12:12-31).

Jesus commanded us to receive the sacrament of Holy Communion regularly in remembrance of him (Luke

22:14-20). And he set the powerful example of service to one another as he washed the feet of the disciples (John 13:1-20).

Worship as the body of Christ—regularly.

Prayer as the body of Christ—fervently.

Service in the body of Christ—faithfully.

How do you contribute to the:

- leadership development and spiritual maturity of the body of Christ?
- ministry and mission of the church in the community around your church?
- ministry and mission of the church in your state and country?
- ministry and mission of your church in the world, which desperately needs the good news of the gospel of Jesus Christ?

Your Mission in the World as a Disciple of Jesus Christ

Jesus commanded us to love God, love our neighbor, and serve others out of this love (John 13:12-20, 34-35). Jesus said, "If you love me, you will keep my commandments. And I will ask the Father, and he will give you another Advocate, to be with you forever" (John 14:15-16).

Jesus' closing words in the Gospel of Matthew are often referred to as the Great Commission. He said: "All authority in heaven and on earth has been given to me. Go therefore and make disciples of all nations, baptizing them in the name of the Father and of the Son and of the Holy Spirit, and teaching them to obey everything that I have commanded you" (Matt. 28:18-20).

The coming of the Holy Spirit on the Day of Pentecost marked the beginning of the church. Peter preached, and the power of God was at work on that day when three thousand people responded to the call to repentance, faith, and Christian discipleship (Acts 2:37-42). We are called to take that same Holy Spirit into our work and our world.

We need Christian study to be able to understand the needs of the world and the needs of those in our community, city, state, and nation. Careful, prayerful study is the foundation for all significant Christian action.

In the book of James we are promised divine wisdom if we "ask God, who gives to all generously and ungrudgingly" (James 1:5). May you see God's wisdom in all your prayer, study, and action.

Remember: Christ is counting on you!

Christian Action

Your Action

What have you done during the past week so Christ will be better known and loved in

- your family?
- your vocation/work?
- your church?
- your community?
- your world?

Reflect on these words:

Christ has no body now on earth but yours,
   no hands but yours;
   no feet but yours.
Yours are the eyes through which the compassion
   of Christ is to look out on a hurting world.
Yours are the feet with which he is to go about doing
   good.
Yours are the hands with which he is to bless now.

—ATTRIBUTED TO SAINT TERESA OF ÁVILA

Web Sites and Ideas for Christian Action

The purpose of Emmaus is to develop servant leaders for the church and for God's mission in the world. You will find beginning ideas at www.upperroom.org/emmaus/servant/.

For additional ideas for appropriate Christian action, consult your Emmaus sponsor, the Community Lay Director, or the Community Spiritual Director. All these people desire to help you grow in grace and to mature in your spiritual life. Don't hesitate to contact them.

Additional ideas for Christian action:

- Volunteer to work in the kitchen at the next Emmaus Walk.
- Volunteer to help in the kitchen at the next Chrysalis Flight or Journey. (Chrysalis is the number one mission outreach of the Walk to Emmaus.)
- Work with your reunion group or accountability group to prepare agape for a future Emmaus or Chrysalis event.
- Prayerfully consider helping with the Kairos prison ministry for adults in prison or the Torch ministry for incarcerated young people.
- Volunteer in a ministry inside the church (for children, youth, or adults).
- Volunteer in a ministry outside the church (food pantry, tutoring program, taking meals to homebound persons, etc.).
- Raise money to help start new Emmaus communities overseas.

The Sacrament of the Lord's Supper

† *The Spiritual Director leading this service should make clear that this is an ecumenical service and everyone is welcome to participate. Those who do not wish to receive the bread and cup for the sake of conscience are still invited to come forward and receive a blessing during the distribution of the elements. Those desiring the blessing instead of the bread and cup may cross their arms over their chest to indicate this desire.*

GREETING

The grace of the Lord Jesus Christ be with you.
And also with you.
The risen Christ is with us!
Praise the Lord!

HYMN OF PRAISE

OPENING PRAYER

**Almighty God, to you all hearts are open,
all desires known,
and from you no secrets are hidden.
Cleanse the thoughts of our hearts
by the inspiration of your Holy Spirit,
that we may perfectly love you,
and worthily magnify your holy name,
through Christ our Lord. Amen.**

PRAYER FOR ILLUMINATION

**Lord, open our hearts and minds
by the power of your Holy Spirit,**

that, as the Scriptures are read
and your Word proclaimed,
we may hear with joy what you say to us today. Amen.

SCRIPTURE

SERMON OR MEDITATION

RESPONSE TO THE WORD
The following or another creed may be used.
I believe in God, the Father Almighty,
creator of heaven and earth.

I believe in Jesus Christ, his only Son, our Lord,
who was conceived by the Holy Spirit,
born of the Virgin Mary,
suffered under Pontius Pilate,
was crucified, died, and was buried;
he descended to the dead.
On the third day he rose again;
he ascended into heaven,
is seated at the right hand of the Father,
and will come again to judge the living and the dead.

I believe in the Holy Spirit,
the holy catholic* church,
the communion of saints,
the forgiveness of sins,
the resurrection of the body,
and the life everlasting. Amen.

universal

CONCERNS AND PRAYERS

† *Brief intercessions, petitions, and thanksgivings may be prayed by the Spiritual Director or spontaneously by members of the congregation. To each of these, all may make a common response, such as: "Lord, hear our prayer."*

INVITATION

Christ our Lord invites to his table all who love him,
    who earnestly repent of their sin
    and seek to live in peace with one another.
Therefore, let us confess our sin before God and one
    another.

CONFESSION AND PARDON

**Merciful God, we confess that we have not loved you
with our whole heart.
We have failed to be an obedient church.
We have not done your will,
we have broken your law,
we have rebelled against your love,
we have not loved our neighbors,
and we have not heard the cry of the needy.
Forgive us, we pray.
Free us for joyful obedience,
through Jesus Christ our Lord. Amen.**

† *All pray in silence*

Hear the good news: Christ died for us while we were yet sinners; that proves God's love toward us. In the name of Jesus Christ, you are forgiven!

In the name of Jesus Christ, you are forgiven!
Glory to God. Amen.

THE PEACE

Let us offer one another signs of reconciliation and love.

† *All, including the Spiritual Director, exchange signs and words of God's peace.*

THE OFFERING

† *The bread and cup are brought to the table at this time if not already present. A hymn, psalm, or anthem may be sung as the offering is received.*

As forgiven and reconciled people,
let us offer ourselves and our gifts to God.

TAKING THE BREAD AND CUP

† *The Spiritual Director, standing if possible behind the Lord's table and facing the people from this time through Breaking the Bread, takes the bread and cup brought by representatives of the people to the Lord's table with the other gifts or uncovers the elements if already in place. Assistant Spiritual Directors may be invited to assist the Spiritual Director in the Great Thanksgiving.*

THE GREAT THANKSGIVING [*all stand*]

The Lord be with you.
And also with you.
Lift up your hearts.
We lift them up to the Lord.

† The Spiritual Director may lift hands and keep them raised.

Let us give thanks to the Lord our God.
It is right to give our thanks and praise.

It is right, and a good and joyful thing,
always and everywhere to give thanks to you,
Father Almighty, creator of heaven and earth.
You formed us in your image
   and breathed into us the breath of life.
When we turned away, and our loved failed,
   your love remained steadfast.
You delivered us from captivity,
   made covenant to be our sovereign God,
   and spoke to us through the prophets.

And so, with your people on earth
and all the company of heaven
we praise your name and join their unending hymn:

*† The Spiritual Director may lower hands. This response and
those that follow may be said or sung.*

Holy, holy, holy Lord, God of power and might,
heaven and earth are full of your glory.
   Hosanna in the highest.
Blessed is he who comes in the name of the Lord.
   Hosanna in the highest.

Holy are you, and blessed is your Son Jesus Christ.
Your Spirit anointed him
   to preach good news to the poor,
   to proclaim release to the captives

and recovering of sight to the blind,
to set at liberty those who are oppressed,
and to announce that the time had come
    when you would save your people.
He healed the sick, fed the hungry, and ate with sinners.
By the baptism of his suffering, death, and resurrection
    you gave birth to your church,
        delivered us from slavery to sin and death,
        and made with us a new covenant
            by water and the Spirit.
When the Lord Jesus ascended,
he promised to be with us always,
    in the power of your Word and Holy Spirit.

† *The Spiritual Director may hold hands, palms down, over the bread; or touch the bread; or lift the bread.*

On the night in which he gave himself up for us,
he took bread, gave thanks to you, broke the bread,
gave it to his disciples, and said:
"Take, eat; this is my body which is given for you.
Do this in remembrance of me."

† *The Spiritual Director may hold hands, palms down, over the cup; or touch the cup; or lift the cup.*

When the supper was over, he took the cup,
    gave thanks to you, gave it to his disciples, and said:
"Drink from this, all of you;
    this is my blood of the new covenant,
    poured out for you and for many
        for the forgiveness of sins.

Do this, as often as you drink it,
in remembrance of me."

† *The Spiritual Director may raise hands.*

And so,
in remembrance of these your mighty acts in
Jesus Christ,
we offer ourselves in praise and thanksgiving
as a holy and living sacrifice,
in union with Christ's offering for us,
as we proclaim the mystery of faith.

Christ has died; Christ is risen; Christ will come again.

† *The Spiritual Director may hold hands, palms down, over the
bread and cup.*

Pour out your Holy Spirit on us gathered here,
and on these gifts of bread and wine.
Make them be for us the body and blood of Christ,
that we may be for the world the body of Christ,
redeemed by his blood.

† *The Spiritual Director may raise his or her hands.*

By your Spirit make us one with Christ,
one with each other,
and one in ministry to all the world,
until Christ comes in final victory
and we feast at his heavenly banquet.

Through your Son Jesus Christ,
with the Holy Spirit in your holy church,

all honor and glory is yours, almighty Father,
now and for ever.
Amen. [† *May be said or sung.*]

THE LORD'S PRAYER

And now, with the confidence of children of God, let us
pray:

† *The Lord's Prayer may be said or sung. If said, either the tra-
ditional or the ecumenical version on page 45 may be used.*

BREAKING THE BREAD

† *The Spiritual Director, still standing behind the Lord's table
facing the people, breaks the bread in silence, or while saying:*

Because there is one loaf, we, who are many,
are one body, for we all partake of the one loaf.
The bread which we break is a sharing in the body of Christ.

† *The Spiritual Director lifts the cup in silence or while saying:*

The cup over which we give thanks is a sharing in the
blood of Christ.

GIVING THE BREAD AND CUP

† *The bread and cup are given to the people, with these or other
words being exchanged:*

The body of Christ, given for you. **Amen.**
The blood of Christ, given for you. **Amen.**

† *The congregation may sing hymns while the bread and cup
are given. When all have received, the Lord's table is put in
order.*

PRAYER AFTER RECEIVING

Eternal God, we give you thanks for this holy mystery
    in which you have given yourself to us.
Grant that we may go into the world
    in the strength of your Spirit,
    to give ourselves for others,
in the name of Jesus Christ our Lord.
    Amen.

HYMN OR SONG

DISMISSAL WITH BLESSING

Go forth in peace.
The grace of the Lord Jesus Christ,
and the love of God,
and the communion of the Holy Spirit
be with you all.
Amen.

De Colores

De co - lo - res, ___ De co - lo-res the fields love to
dress in all dur-ing the spring-time. De co - lo - res, _
_ De co - lo - res the birds have their clo-thing that
comes ev-'ry sea-son. De co - lo - res, ___ De co -
lo-res the rain-bow is vest-ed a - cross the blue sky.

Chorus

De co - lo - res, and so must all love be of

(Repeat)

ev - 'ry bright col - or to make my heart cry.

*This song is part of the Emmaus tradition. The author and composer are unknown.

Words and Resources for Singing

De Colores (author unknown)

> De colores,
> De colores, the fields love to dress in
>   all during the springtime.
> De colores,
> De colores the birds have their clothing
>   that comes every season.
> De colores,
> De colores the rainbow is vested
>   across the blue sky.

Chorus:
> **De colores, and so must all love be**
> **of every bright color**
> **to make my heart cry.** *(Repeat)*

De colores,
De colores we witness the sunup
   on clear and bright mornings.

De colores,
De colores the sun gives its treasures
   God's light to God's children.

De colores the diamond will sparkle
   when brought to the light.

Chorus *(above)*

De Colores

¡De colores!
De colores se visten los campos
   en la primavera.
¡De colores!
De colores son los pajarillos
   que vienen de afuera.
¡De colores!
De colores es el arcoiris
   que vemos lucir.

Coro:
Y por eso los grandes amores
de muchos colores
   me gustan a mí. *(Se repite)*

¡De colores!
De colores brillantes y finos
   se viste la aurora.

¡De colores!
De colores son los mil reflejos
   que el sol atesora.
¡De colores!
De colores se viste el diamante
   que vemos lucir.

Coro:
Y por eso los grandes amores
de muchos colores
   me gustan a mí. *(Se repite)*

Sings the rooster,
Sings the rooster with his *quiri, quiri, quiri, quiri, quiri.*

And the cluck-hen,
And the cluck-hen with her *cara, cara, cara, cara, cara.*

And the babe-chicks,
And the babe-chicks with their *pio, pio, pio, pio, pio.*

De colores and so must all love be,
of every bright color
to make my heart cry. *(Repeat)*

¡Canta el gallo!
Canta el gallo con el quiri, quiri, quiri, quiri, quiri.

La gallina,
La gallina con el cara, cara, cara, cara, cara.

Los polluelos,
Los polluelos con el pío, pío, pío, pío, pi.

Y por eso los grandes amores
de muchos colores
me gustan a mí. *(Se repite)*

Sing Alleluia to the Lord

Sing alleluia to the Lord.
Sing alleluia to the Lord.
Sing alleluia,
Sing alleluia,
Sing alleluia to the Lord.

Jesus, Jesus

Jesus, Jesus, can I tell you how I feel?
You have given me your Spirit, I love you so.

Source Unknown

Christ Has Died

Christ has died, Alleluia.
Christ is risen, Alleluia.
Christ will come again,
Alleluia, alleluia.

Mealtime Blessings

Blessing before Meals*

Gathered at this table, Holy Spirit, come!
Fill us with your presence, bind our hearts as one.
Bless this time together; Jesus, give us peace.
Come, Lord, be with us, join us as we meet.
Come, Lord, be with us, bless this food we eat.

Blessing after Meals*

As we leave this table, fed by your own hand,
Holy Spirit, fill us, 'til we meet again.
Jesus, as we leave here, let us walk your way,
sharing God's blessings, as we do and say,
sharing forever, your love here today.

*Words by Gary Mattingly. Copyright © 2004 Upper Room Ministries. All rights reserved. Music for the mealtime blessings may be downloaded as audio and print files at: emmaus.upperroom.org

Wesley's Grace**

Be present at our table, Lord;
Be here and everywhere adored.
Thy mercies bless, and grant that we
May feast in fellowship with thee. Amen.

**Sung to the tune of the "Doxology" or "Old 100th"

Whom Do You Trust?

Read Romans: 4:13-22

The LORD answered Job: "Where were you when I laid the foundation of the earth? Tell me, if you have understanding."

—Job 38:1, 4

All my life I had been a modern-day Pharisee. It was important to me and my security to know what to believe in, what the right doctrine was, which preacher had the "truth," which church was correct.

In my mind I played a game in which I thought I would be at peace if I figured out the "truth." This "truth" would often change from day to day, but I still played the game—to my own detriment. Finally I heard the voice of God saying to me, "Why torture yourself? You do not know all the answers, and you never will. I do know the answers, and I can be trusted."

I did not listen right away. I kept asking my questions: "How was the universe made? How can I know the Bible is true?" To every question came the same answer, "Trust me."

"But God—" I would say.

"Trust me," God would answer. "I need proof!" I would respond.

"You need me," God would reply.

It is slowly sinking in. No doctrine saves me. Not even the Bible does. God saves me.

Tim Burleson (South Carolina)

Prayer: Thank you, Father, that I have you. Today I place my trust in you anew, through Jesus Christ our Lord. Amen.

Thought for the Day

Our trust is in the Lord.

Prayer Focus: Those who need proof to believe

Now I Know
Read John 3:11-21

There is salvation in no one else, for there is no other name under heaven given among mortals by which we must be saved.

—Acts 4:12

A patient, Rehana, needed testing to confirm a tuberculosis diagnosis. I suggested that she come to the Leprosy Mission Hospital the next day for a blood test. She stared at my face and said, "I will not be able to go to your leprosy hospital. If anyone from my village sees me going there, they will think that I too have leprosy."

I know about the stigma associated with leprosy; Rehana feared banishment from her village. I informed her that it was no longer only a leprosy hospital but was a general hospital treating most ailments. I could see an expression of hope in her face. Rehana replied, "I did not know this. Now I know, and I will come tomorrow."

I understand Rehana's perspective—and her relief. For years I believed that Christ came to the world for only a particular group of people. I often envied these people for having such a loving God who came down from heaven to deliver them from their bondage to sin. But one day, while attending a gospel meeting, I came to know that Jesus died for the sins of the whole world. I was overwhelmed when someone shared with me the words in Acts 4:12, and I accepted Jesus as my personal Savior. Knowing Christ has changed my life.

Pramila Barkataki (Uttar Pradesh, India)

Prayer: Redeeming God, help us to share the good news of Christ with those around us. Amen.

Thought for the Day
How has knowing Christ changed my life?
Prayer Focus: Those served by mission hospitals

Hold the Ladder

Read 1 Corinthians 12:12-27

The members of the body that seem to be weaker are indispensable.
—1 Corinthians 12:22

Recently, a mission group came to our church to repair the building. Several of us offered to help carry water, haul sand, lay brick, or paint. When work assignments were posted, mine was to hold the ladder for the painter. A bit disappointed, I wished for something more challenging and important. Soon I observed how difficult and dangerous it was to paint the high walls of the church, and I realized that what I was doing was important. Fulfilling my task ensured that the painter could safely do his job.

This helped me understand how much the leaders of the church rely on people to "hold the ladder." These supporters who are rarely seen and are not widely known by others may feel insignificant. Yet their prayers and vigils on behalf of the pastor and other leaders create an invisible wall of support and surround leaders with strength and protection.

For the many who are recognized in taking the lead for the kingdom of God, there are lesser recognized but equal counterparts and partners in service who support these folk. Where there are highly visible leaders doing wonderful work for God, we can be sure there are some people like me that day—"holding the ladder" for them.

Roberto Herrera Betancourt (Holguín, Cuba)

Prayer: O God, thank you for those who are called to intercede on behalf of leaders and who support them. Amen.

Thought for the Day

All members of the body of Christ are important.
Prayer Focus: Those who pray for our leaders

The Upper Room as Your Fourth-Day Devotional Guide

Daily time with God was at the heart of Jesus' life of prayer, and the same is true of those of us whose hearts now burn with the fire of his love. The meditations on the three previous pages were taken from *The Upper Room* daily devotional guide.

If you do not already have a daily guide to prayer for your Fourth-Day spiritual practice, we invite you to consider using *The Upper Room*. You can find it online at

www.upperroom.org

and choose to read it there free of charge every day. Or you can sign up to receive the daily devotion by e-mail. Or you can subscribe to the printed version for a special discount of 30 percent.

Special Offer!

Have one year (6 issues) of *The Upper Room* delivered to your home at 30 percent off the subscription price!

To order, call **1-800-972-0433**
and mention this discount code: **EMMAUS**

The Lord's Prayer (Traditional Version)

Our Father, who art in heaven,
hallowed be thy name.
Thy kingdom come,
thy will be done on earth as it is in heaven.
Give us this day our daily bread.
And forgive us our trespasses,
as we forgive those who trespass against us.
And lead us not into temptation,
but deliver us from evil.
For thine is the kingdom, and the power, and the glory,
forever. Amen.

The Lord's Prayer (Ecumenical Version)

Our Father in heaven,
hallowed be your name,
your kingdom come,
your will be done, on earth as in heaven.
Give us today our daily bread.
Forgive us our sins
as we forgive those who sin against us.
Save us from the time of trial
and deliver us from evil.
For the kingdom, the power, and the glory are yours
now and for ever. Amen.

Pattern for Prayer

There are many patterns for prayer, whether they are used in the morning or evening. In time your own pattern will develop. Until your own pattern emerges, consider using the following approach; you can remember it easily because it spells the word *ACTS*.

Begin by finding a quiet place and centering yourself in God's presence.

Adoration

Adoration is the second movement of prayer. To adore God is to worship and praise God in your heart, in your mind, and with your lips. Read aloud Psalm 100 (page 6). Then take a few minutes to praise and adore God in your own words.

Confession

Next, move to confession as you examine yourself and clarify your vision of who you are before God. Begin at the personal level, and then confess the sins of your church, community, and nation.

Thanksgiving

After the movement of confession come prayers of thanksgiving, which overflow from gratitude. Recall specific things for which you want to thank God.

Supplication

Adoration, confession, and thanksgiving have prepared you for supplication. Supplication is the combination of intercession and petition—a remembering of things hoped for. In your heart, name specific persons and needs for which you seek God's help. Bring these needs and persons into God's presence in prayer.

Close your prayer with commitment, in your own words, asking God to send the Holy Spirit to enable a new creation to come alive in you.

Order of the Group Reunion

Prayer to the Holy Spirit (see page 48)

1. **Review your Group Reunion Card:**
   Prayer, Study, Action.

2. **Closest to Christ**
   At what moment this past week did you feel closest to Christ?

3. **Call to Discipleship**
   At what moment during this week did you feel you were responding to God's call to be a disciple? Where did you participate this week in being the church, the heartbeat of Christ?

4. **Discipleship Denied**
   When was your faith tested this week through failure?

5. **Your Plan**
   What is your plan for prayer, study, and action for the week to come?

6. **Reunion Group Activities**

7. **Prayers for Special Needs**
   Pray for those who are absent.

8. **Prayer of Thanksgiving** (see page 48)

Prayer to the Holy Spirit

Come, Holy Spirit,
  fill the hearts of your faithful
  and kindle in us the fire of your love.
Send forth your Spirit, and we shall be created.
And you shall renew the face of the earth.

O God, who by the light of the Holy Spirit
  did instruct the hearts of the faithful,
  grant that by the same Holy Spirit
  we may be truly wise
  and ever enjoy your consolations.
Through Christ our Lord. Amen.

Prayer of Thanksgiving

Almighty God, who lives and reigns forever,
we give you thanks
for all the gifts you have bestowed upon us. Amen.

CPSIA information can be obtained
at www.ICGtesting.com
Printed in the USA
JSHW031603070920
7665JS00003B/3

9 780835 815123